Easy Homemade Brea
50 simple and delicious
Bakery Cooking Series

Bread making is not a common household chore like it was many years ago. Making bread doesn't have to be a time consuming and daunting task. On your first attempts at making homemade bread you might feel it is a very long and tedious task but once you learn the art of bread making, you will love having fresh homemade bread. Not only is this so much better for you then store-bought bread, you can do a lot with homemade bread dough.

We've included some of our favorite recipes that will surely fill your house with that fresh baked bread smell.

Included in this Homemade Bread Recipes Cookbook:
10 quick bread recipes
10 white and whole wheat yeast bread recipes
10 bread mixer recipes
10 bread sticks and rolls recipes
10 recipes and ideas of what to do with bread dough beyond a loaf of bread. (We are talking meals and desserts you can make with bread dough!)

Table of Contents

Quick Breads

Quick breads are breads that don't have to rise. These include many variations of vegetable or fruit breads such as banana, zucchini, carrot, pumpkin, etc. They also freeze well so make extra for the freezer!

Banana Bread
Ingredients

1 1/2 Cups white sugar
3/4 Cup butter, softened or shortening
4 eggs
4 mashed bananas
1/2 tsp. Soda
3 1/2 Cups flour
1 tsp. salt
1 tsp. vanilla extract
1 Cup chopped pecans, if desired

Directions

Grease two loaf pans and set aside. In separate small bowl, mash bananas and stir in baking soda. In mixer, cream together white sugar and butter.

Add eggs, salt, and vanilla. Blend until creamy. Add flour and blend until well combined. Stir in banana mixture and nuts and stir gently to combine.

Bake in a 350-degree oven for 45-50 minutes or until a toothpick inserted in the middle of the loaf comes out clean.

Chocolate Chip Banana Bread

Ingredients
3/4 Cup white sugar
2 tsp. baking powder
1/4 Cup butter, melted
1/4 tsp. baking soda
2 eggs
2 Cups white flour
1 Cup chopped nuts, optional
1 Cup mashed bananas, about 2-3
3/4 Cup chocolate chips

Directions
Grease 1 loaf pan and set aside. In mixer, cream together butter, sugar and eggs. Add flour and blend well.

Add mashed bananas, baking powder, salt, baking soda and mix gently until combined. Gently fold in nuts and chips.

Bake loaf in the oven at 350 degrees for about 60 minutes or until toothpick inserted in the middle comes out clean.

Applesauce Bread
Ingredients
1/2 Cup butter, softened
1 Cup white sugar
1 egg
1 1/4 Cups applesauce
1 1/2 Cups white flour
1 1/2 tsp. Soda
1 tsp. Cinnamon
3/4 tsp. Nutmeg
1/2 tsp. Salt
1/4 tsp. ground cloves
1/2 Cup raisins, optional
1/2 Cup chopped nuts, optional

Directions
Grease loaf pan and preheat oven to 350 degrees. In mixer, cream butter and sugar together. Then add egg and applesauce. Blend together.

In separate bowl, stir together flour, baking soda, cinnamon, nutmeg, salt and cloves. Pour gently into mixer and mix until well combined.

Gently fold in raisins and nuts, if desired. Pour into loaf pan. Bake about 50-55 minutes.

Pumpkin Bread
Ingredients
1 Cup canned pumpkin
2 eggs
1/2 Cup milk
1 Cup shortening
1 Cup brown sugar
2 Cups flour
1 tsp. Cinnamon
1 tsp. cloves
1/4 tsp. Nutmeg
1/4 tsp. Baking soda
1 T. baking powder
1/4 tsp. Salt
1/2 Cup chopped nuts, optional
1/2 Cup raisins
Directions
Grease two loaf pans and preheat oven at 350 degrees.

In mixer, add pumpkin, milk, eggs, shortening and brown sugar. Cream together. Blend in flour, brown sugar, cinnamon, salt, baking soda, baking powder, nutmeg and cloves.

Blend together until creamy. Gently stir in chopped nuts and raisins, if using. Pour batter into prepared loaf pans. Bake for 60 minutes.

Best if you let sit several hours or overnight before eating.

Zucchini Bread

Ingredients
2 Cups grated zucchini
3 eggs
1 Cup oil
2 Cups white sugar
3 tsp. vanilla
3 Cups flour
1 tsp. baking soda
1/4 tsp. baking powder
1 tsp. Salt
3 tsp. Cinnamon

Directions
Grease loaf pan and preheat oven to 350 degrees.
In mixer, blend together eggs, sugar, oil and vanilla.
Add shredded zucchini.

In a separate bowl, add dry ingredients; flour, baking soda, baking powder, salt and cinnamon. Slowly add the dry ingredients into the wet ingredients stirring gently.

Pour into loaf pan(s). Bake for 45-50 minutes.

Coconut Pumpkin Nut Bread

Ingredients

2 Cups packed dark brown sugar
2/3 Cup white sugar
1 (15 ounce) can pumpkin puree
1 Cup vegetable oil
2/3 Cup coconut milk
3 1/2 *cups* all-purpose flour
2 tsp. baking soda
1 tsp. salt
1 1/2 tsp. ground cinnamon
1 tsp. ground nutmeg
2/3 Cup flaked coconut
1 Cup chopped pecans, optional

Directions

Grease 2 loaf pans and preheat oven at 350 degrees F. In large bowl, blend dry ingredients together including flour, baking soda, salt, nutmeg and cinnamon. Set aside.

In mixer, cream together white and brown sugars, pumpkin, oil, and coconut milk. Mix until well blended. Add in dry ingredients and mix together.

Gently stir in shredded coconut and chopped nuts. Pour into loaf pans. Bake for about 1 hour or until a toothpick inserted in the middle of the loaf comes out clean.

Blueberry Bread

Ingredients
2 Cups flour
1 Cups sugar
1 tsp. Baking powder
1/2 tsp. Baking soda
1/2 tsp. Salt
1/4 Cups butter, cold
2/3 Cups buttermilk
2 tsp. Vanilla
1 egg, beaten
1 Cup fresh blueberries

Directions
Preheat oven at 350 degrees F. Grease one loaf pan. In mixer add together flour, sugar, baking powder, baking soda and salt. With pastry blender, cut in 1/4 cup cold butter until crumbly.

Add buttermilk, vanilla and egg into crumbly mixture. Stir until just moist. Gently stir in blueberries with a spoon. Pour into greased pan.

Bake for one hour or until toothpick inserted in center comes out clean.

Carrot Bread
Ingredients
3 eggs
2 Cups white sugar
1 Cup canola oil
1 Cup grated carrot
1 small can crushed pineapple, about 1 Cup, don't
drain
2 tsp vanilla
2 Cups flour
1 tsp salt
1 tsp baking soda
1 1/2 tsp cinnamon
1 Cup chopped nuts, optional
1/2 Cup raisins, optional

Directions
Grease 2 loaf pans and preheat oven to 350 degrees.
In large bowl, blend dry ingredients together including
flour, salt, baking soda, and cinnamon.

In mixer, cream together sugar, oil, vanilla and eggs.
Slowly blend in dry ingredients into the wet. Gently stir
in carrots, pineapple, nuts and raisins.

Pour into loaf pans and bake about 1 hour until
toothpick inserted in center comes out clean.

Lemon Bread

Ingredients

1 Cup sugar
2 eggs
6 Tablespoons butter
Grated rind of one lemon
1/2 Cup milk
1 1/2 Cup flour
1 tsp. baking powder
1/4 tsp. salt

Directions

Preheat oven to 350 degrees and grease one loaf pan.

In mixer, cream together sugar, butter, and eggs. Add in lemon zest, milk, flour, baking powder and salt. Blend until smooth. Pour into a greased loaf pan.

Bake for one hour or until toothpick inserted in center comes out clean.

Cranberry Orange Bread
Ingredients
1/4 Cup butter, melted or soft
3/4 Cup orange juice
3/4 Cup white sugar
2 eggs
2 Cups flour
2 tsp baking powder
1/2 tsp baking soda
1 teaspoon salt
1 T. orange zest
1 Cup dried cranberries
1/2 Cup chopped nuts, optional

Directions
In mixer, blend together butter, orange juice, white sugar and eggs until creamy. Add in flour, baking powder, baking soda, salt and orange zest. Blend together. Hand stir in cranberries and nuts.

Pour into a greased loaf pan and bake in a preheated 350 degrees oven for 1 hour or until toothpick inserted in the middle comes out clean.

White and Whole Wheat Yeast Breads

Here are a few secrets to making homemade bread:

One to make it when you have a lot of time, perhaps on the weekend. It isn't a hard thing to do, but it can be time consuming. Once you mix the dough, you'll need to let it sit for at least one hour to rise and double. Then come back and place it into loaf pans and let it sit again. Then bake it.

This is why a lot of people don't like to make homemade bread but I find it works great to mix the dough together, set a timer, and work on other projects around the house while the dough is doing its thing. We've also included a shorter version that will be done quicker, if you prefer!

The **second** secret is to make sure your water or liquid you are using in the recipe is warm, not burning hot or too cold, but warm to the touch. This will help your yeast to bubble and make your dough rise.

Third, use a large mixer such as a Kitchen Aid or Bosch for anything that has more than 5 Cups of flour. This can be a very big dough to mix otherwise. If you don't have a large mixer, you can cut the recipe in half to make it easier to manage. Of course, you can always make bread dough in a large bowl and a large spoon to stir. It will be a great arm exercise!

Common Bread Baking Questions
Why does bread have to rise so long?

It is all about the chemistry here. The yeast helps the bread to rise gives your baked bread a light, airy texture.

Why do you knead bread dough?

This helps the gluten in the bread to bind the ingredients together as well as creating air pockets that will help the bread to rise.

Why grease the bowl the bread is going to rise in?

Once you get done mixing your dough, you will knead the dough and place in a greased bowl for rising. This is done by adding a small swirl of oil into a large bowl. Swirl the bowl around to cover the bottom and edges. Place your dough in the oil and flip it over to coat both sides. While the dough is rising it will move up the sides of the bowl and grow, oiling the bowl helps this process.

White Bread

Ingredients

6 Cups water
6 Tablespoons sugar
6 Tablespoons shortening
2 Tablespoons salt
3 Tablespoons honey
2 pkgs yeast
1/2 Cup warm water
1 teaspoon sugar

Directions

In small bowl or cup, add 2 packages of yeast and 1/2 Cup water. Sprinkle in 1 teaspoon sugar. Set aside. In microwave safe bowl, add water, sugar, honey, salt and shortening.

Heat 2 minutes until warmed. Pour into mixer bowl. Allow to cool if mixture is hot you want it to be warm to the touch but not overly hot or it will kill the yeast. Add in yeast mixture.

Slowly add in flour until mixture becomes a smooth ball of dough. About 8 Cups of flour but add one cup at a time until reach a nice consistency. Take out of mixer and knead on a clean surface several minutes. Place in an oiled bowl and let sit 1 hour.

Punch dough down and let rise again 30 minutes. Form into 3-4 loaves, depending on size you'd like. Let rest 15 minutes and bake at 350 degrees for about 40 minutes.

Whole Wheat Bread
Ingredients
6 Cups warm water
2 T. yeast
2/3 Cup honey
2/3 Cup oil
3 T. molasses
1 Cup oats
2 T. salt
6 Cups whole wheat flour

Directions
In a small bowl, add one cup warm water and yeast. Sprinkle with a pinch of sugar. In mixer bowl, add oats, honey, oil, molasses and salt. Add 2 cups flour and blend together. Pour in yeast mixture. Continue adding one cup a flour at a time until well combined and dough pulls away from sides of mixer bowl.

Spread oil along sides of two large bowls, or spray with cooking spray. Divide dough in half and place each half in a greased bowl. Cover with a clean towel and let rise for one hour.

Grease 5 bread pans and divide dough into equal portions. Place one in each pan and allow to rise until dough reaches the top of the bread pan. Cook in a preheated oven at 350 degrees for about 30 minutes

French Baguettes

Ingredients

2 cups warm water
2 Tablespoons vegetable oil
3 teaspoons salt
2 Tablespoons sugar
2 Tablespoons yeast dissolved in 1 Cup warm water
7-7 1/2 Cups flour
Cornmeal, optional
Egg, beaten

Directions

Add yeast to 1 cup warm water and add in sugar. Set aside. In mixer, remaining water, oil and, 3 teaspoons salt. Add in 2 cups of the flour to the mixer. Blend together. Add yeast with the water. Slowly blend and add in one cup a flour at a time. Dough will start to pull away from sides of the mixer.

If too sticky, blend in 1/4-1/2 Cup flour until dough ball forms. Place on clean counter and knead several minutes. Separate dough into two equal portions and continue to knead until dough feels soft and pliable.

Add oil to two large bowls and place a ball of dough in each. Flip the dough over so both sides of the dough have been greased. Cover with a clean towel and let rise for one hour.

Spray or grease a cookie sheet. Sprinkle with cornmeal. Roll each ball of dough into a rectangle. Roll up jelly roll style. Seal the ends and place on cookie sheet. Cut diagonal slits on the top of each loaf. Let sit again one hour.

Before cooking brush, a beaten egg onto each loaf. Bake for 15-20 minutes until golden brown.

If you want smaller individual loaves divide the two halves into smaller pieces.

90 Minute Bread

Ingredients
1/2 Cup sugar
1/4 Cup shortening, melted
4 Cups warm water
4 teaspoons salt
4 pkgs. Yeast
7-8 Cups flour

Directions
In a mixer bowl, dissolve sugar in warm water and add in yeast. Let sit several minutes. Add remaining ingredients and blend together to make a soft dough.

Blend until dough starts to pull away from sides of mixer. Place dough on a floured surface and knead several minutes. Divide dough into four pieces and let rest 15 minutes, covered.

Grease 4 loaf pans and place a ball of dough into each pan. Let rest in pans for 15 minutes. Bake in a preheated oven at 375 for 30 minutes until golden brown.

Wheat Bread

Ingredients
3 Tablespoons yeast
5 1/2 Cup water
2 T salt
2/3 Cup oil
2/3 Cup honey
3/4 Cup gluten
12 Cups wheat flour or more if needed

Directions
Add yeast to 1 Cup water and sprinkle with a pinch of sugar. This helps feed the yeast.

In a mixer, add salt, oil, honey, gluten and two cups of flour. Blend together. Add in yeast mixture and continue to mix, adding one cup of flour at a time until dough starts to form a ball and pulls away from sides.

Take out of mixer and knead on a floured surface several minutes until soft and smooth. Place dough in a floured bowl and let rise one hour covered with a towel or plastic wrap.

Divide dough in equal portions, however many loaves you'd like. (I usually do 5) Let rise in bread pans 15 minutes or until dough rises to the top edge of the pan. Bake in a preheated oven at 350 degrees for 30 minutes.

Depending on the size of the loaf, you may need a longer cooking time.

Molasses Whole Wheat Bread

Ingredients
2 T yeast dissolved in 1/2 cup warm water
5 cup hot water
7 cups whole wheat flour
1/3 cup honey
1/3 cup molasses
2/3 cup oil
3/4 Cup gluten, you can leave out if you don't have available
2 T salt

Directions
5-6 more cups of flour; whole wheat or white
In mixer bowl, combine water, 7 cups of wheat flour, honey, molasses, oil and salt. Beat for about one minute until well combined. Sprinkle in yeast and continue to blend together. Add in gluten if using and flour, one cup at a time.

This makes a large amount of dough so you may need to finish mixing by hand or kneading on the counter. Knead about 5 minutes until dough is soft and pliable. Let rest in a greased bowl for one hour.

Shape into loaves or place into 4-5 bread pans. Let rest an additional 15-20 minutes. Bake in a preheated oven about 40 minutes depending on the size of your loaves.

Honey Wheat Bread

Dissolve:
4 1/2 teaspoons Yeast
1/2 Cup water

In mixing bowl mix:
4 Cups warm water
1/2 Cup oil
2 Tablespoons salt
2/3 Cup honey

Then add in yeast mixture.
Add 4-5 Cups whole wheat flour to mixture. Continue adding flour until dough forms a nice ball and mixture pulls away from sides of the bowl.
You will need a total of 6 Cups wheat flour and 2 Cups white flour.

Knead dough and let rise until doubles.
Separate into 4 balls and cover with a towel or plastic wrap. Let rise 20 minutes.
Bake at 350 degrees for 25-30 minutes.

White & Wheat Bread
Ingredients
1 Tablespoon yeast
2 1/2 Cups warm water
3 Tablespoons sugar
1/4 Cup +2 T. dry milk powder
3 Tablespoons butter, melted
1 Tablespoon salt
2 Cups wheat flour
4-6 cups white flour

Directions
In mixer bowl, add in warm water and yeast. Sprinkle sugar on the top and let sit one minute. Add in milk powder, melted butter, salt and 2 Cups wheat flour. Blend together. Continue mixing adding one cup of flour at a time until a ball of dough forms and pulls away from sides of mixer.

Add dough to an oiled bowl and let rise one hour. Divide into 4 loaves and place in loaf pans. Cover and let rise additional 20 minutes. Bake in a preheated 350-degree oven for 30 minutes.

Yeast Bread in a Bag

This is a fun recipe for kids to create. I used this recipe in an afterschool cooking class where they could have their own Ziploc bag and then place the dough in their individual loaf pan.

Ingredients
2 Cups white flour
1 Cup wheat flour
1 Tablespoon or 1 package of yeast
3 Tablespoons dry milk
1 teaspoon salt
Add ingredients in a large Ziploc bag. Squeeze air out of bag and seal tight. Mix together. Open bag and add in:
1 Cup warm water
3 Tablespoons oil

Directions
Squeeze air out of bag again and seal tight. Mix together by squeezing ingredients together through bag. Dust clean counter with flour and take bread dough out of bag. Knead dough on floured surface. Let sit for 10-15 minutes.

Then shape dough into a loaf and place in sprayed loaf pan. Cover and let rise 30 minutes. Bake at 375 degrees for 25-30 minutes or until golden brown.

Croissants

Ingredients
5 Cups flour
1 1/2 Cups butter, cold
1 Cup warm water
1 tablespoon yeast or a packet
3/4 Cup half and half
1/3 Cup sugar
2 eggs
1 1/2 teaspoons salt
1/4 Cup butter, melted
1 tablespoon water

Directions
In mixer add 1 Cup cold butter that has been cut in to slices and 4 cups of the flour. Mix together until mixture is crumbly. Set to the side.

In a small glass, add yeast in warm water. Sprinkle sugar on top of the yeast and let sit several minutes. When yeast starts to foam pour into empty mixing bowl. Stir in 1 cup flour, 1/3 cup sugar, melted butter, half and half, 1 egg, and salt. Mix together until ingredients form a ball. Chill several hours.

Divide dough into 4 balls of dough. Knead each several minutes. Roll one ball of dough into a large circle. Cut into triangles. Roll each triangle up starting at the wide edge. Ending with the pointed end up. Bend ends to look like a crescent shape.

Place on an ungreased cookie sheet and finish rolling remaining dough. Cover with a towel and let rise 1-2 hours. Before baking, beat one egg with 1 tablespoon water and brush each croissant with egg wash. Bake at 325 degrees for 25-30 minutes or until golden brown.

To **add fillings to croissants, place a tablespoon of filling on triangle before rolling up. Fillings could include chopped fruit, jam, chocolate chunk, cooked chicken mixture or a cream filling.

Bread Mixer Recipes

Italian Bread

Ingredients
1 Cup warm milk
1 egg
2 T. butter, melted
1/4 Cup white sugar
1 tsp salt
3 Cups white flour
2 tsp. yeast

Directions
Add ingredients into bread pan as listed and select dough setting. Split dough in half and place in 8-inch round pan. Cover with a towel or plastic wrap. Let rise 30-45 minutes until dough fills the pan.

Beat one egg and 1 Tablespoon water together and brush on to each circle of dough. Sprinkle with Italian seasoning and garlic salt.

Bake at 350 degrees for 20 minutes until golden brown.

Sour Cream Vanilla Bread
Ingredients
1/2 Cup warm water
1 T. vanilla
1/3 Cup sour cream
1 egg
1 T. butter, soft
3 T. sugar
3 Cups bread flour
1 1/4 tsp. salt
2 tsp. yeast

Directions
Add ingredients in order listed and bake in bread machine.

Golden Egg Bread
Ingredients
3/4 Cup water
3 T. sugar
3 T. vegetable oil
2 eggs
1 1/2 tsp. Salt
3 1/2 Cups flour
2 tsp. Yeast or one package

Directions
Place all ingredients in bread machine in order. Bake according to bread machine instructions.

Cheese and Onion Bread

Ingredients

1 1/3 Cups water
3 T. dry milk powder
1 1/2 teaspoons salt
2 T. white sugar
3 2/3 Cups white flour
1 T. dried onion
1/3 Cup shredded cheddar cheese
1 1/4 teaspoon yeast

Directions

Place all ingredients in bread machine in order. Bake according to bread machine instructions.

Italian Herb Bread
Ingredients
1 1/3 Cups water
3 T. dry milk powder
1 1/2 teaspoons salt
3 T. white sugar
3 T. shortening
3 3/4 Cups white flour
1 1/2 tsp. basil
1 1/2 tsp Italian seasoning or mixed herbs
2 tsp yeast

Directions
Place all ingredients in bread machine in order. Bake according to bread machine instructions.

Cheese & Herb Bread
Ingredients

1 1/3 cups water warm
2 T. butter softened
1/2 tsp salt
3 tsp sugar
1 tsp parsley
1/2 tsp basil
3 Cups flour
1 Cup whole wheat flour
3 tsp yeast
2/3 Cup cheddar cheese
1/4 Cup parmesan cheese

Directions
Place all ingredients in bread machine in order. Bake according to bread machine instructions.

Cheese Herb Sandwich Rolls

Ingredients

1/4 Cup warm water
1/4 Cup warm milk
1 egg
2/3 Cup cottage cheese
1/4 Cup grated Parmesan cheese
3 T. sugar
1 1/2 tsp salt
3 Cups white flour
2 1/4 tsp active dry yeast or one packet
1 tsp Italian seasoning
1/2 tsp dried minced garlic
1/4 tsp dried basil
1/4 Cup chopped onion
4 1/2 tsp butter

Directions

Add butter to frying pan and sauté onion. Set aside. Place all other ingredients in bread machine in order. Press dough cycle. After 5 minutes of mixing add in sautéed onions. When cycle is done, divide into as many rolls as you'd like. Place on a cookie sheet and let rise 30 minutes. Bake rolls in a 350-preheated oven for about 10-15 minutes until golden brown.

Cinnamon Swirl Bread

Ingredients

1 Cup warm milk
1/4 Cup water
2 eggs
1/4 Cup butter, melted
1 tsp. salt
1/4 Cup sugar
5 Cups flour
2 1/4 teaspoons active dry yeast

Directions

Place all ingredients in bread machine in order. Select dough setting. Divide dough in half and cover the one you are not working with. Roll dough into a rectangle. Brush with butter and filling below:

FILLING:

2 T. butter, melted
1/3 Cup sugar
1 T. ground cinnamon

Sprinkle sugar and cinnamon on to melted butter. Roll up jelly roll style. Pinch ends and lay on a greased loaf pan.

Continue with other ball of dough. Cover with a light towel and let loaves rise one hour.

Bake for 25-30 minutes until golden brown.

Take out of pans and drizzle glaze over each loaf.

GLAZE:

1 Cup confectioners' sugar
4 to 5 tsp. milk
1/2 tsp. vanilla extract

When cycle is completed, turn dough onto a lightly floured surface; divide in half. Roll each portion into a 10-in. x 8-in. rectangle. Brush with butter. Combine sugar and cinnamon; sprinkle over dough. Roll up tightly jelly-roll style, starting with a short side. Pinch seams and ends to seal.

Place seam side down in two greased 9-in. x 5-in. x 3-in. loaf pans. Cover and let rise in a warm place until doubled, about 1 hour. Bake at 350 degrees for 25 minutes. Cover with foil; bake 5-10 minutes longer or until golden brown. Remove from pans to wire racks to cool completely.

Pepperoni Bread

Ingredients
1 Cup + 2 T. water
1/3 Cup shredded mozzarella cheese
2 T. sugar
1 1/2 tsp. Garlic salt
1 1/2 tsp. dried oregano
3 1/4 Cup flour
1 1/2 tsp. Yeast
2/3 Cup pepperoni, chopped

Directions
In bread machine, add all ingredients except pepperoni. Just before the final kneading cycle, your machine may audibly signal this, add the pepperoni.

Double Chocolate Chip Loaf

Ingredients
1 Cup water
1 (1 oz.) square of bittersweet chocolate, melted and cooled to room temperature
1 egg
3 tbsp of honey
1 1/2 tsp salt
3 1/4 Cup bread flour
1/3 Cup buttermilk powder
2 tbsp unsweetened cocoa powder, sifted
1 1/2 tsp instant yeast
1/2 Cup chocolate chips

Directions
In bread machine, add all ingredients except chocolate chips. Select sweet dough cycle. Just before the final kneading cycle, your machine may audibly signal this, add the chocolate chips.

Rolls and Breadsticks

Overnight Rolls

Ingredients
1 Tablespoon yeast
1 Cup warm water
1/2 Cup butter, melted
2 eggs
1 tsp salt
4 Cups white flour

Directions
In small bowl, add warm water and add in yeast and a sprinkle of sugar. Set aside. In a mixer bowl, add melted butter, eggs, salt and two cups flour. Blend together. Add in yeast mixture and two more cups flour. Knead dough several minutes on a floured counter. Let sit overnight covered with plastic wrap.

Next day, roll balls of dough into rolls and place on cookie sheet. Let rest 20 minutes. Bake at 375 degrees for 12-15 minutes until golden brown.

Dinner Rolls

Ingredients
4 1/2 Cups flour
1 pkg. yeast
1 Cup milk
1/3 Cup sugar
1/3 Cup. butter, melted
1 tsp. salt
2 eggs

Directions
In a saucepan, heat milk, sugar and butter. Warm stirring continually until sugar dissolves and butter is melted. Let cool off slightly if too hot.

In mixer bowl, add milk mixture, salt, 2 Cups flour and eggs. Blend together. Add in in remaining flour. Knead into a large bowl and place in a greased bowl. Cover and let sit for 1 hour.

Shape dough into rolls and place on a cookie sheet. Let rise additional 20-30 minutes. Bake in a preheat 375 degrees oven for 12-15 minutes until golden brown.

Potato Rolls
Ingredients
8 Cups flour
2 T. sugar
4 teaspoons salt
2 T. yeast
1/4 Cup butter
2 eggs
1/2 Cup water
1 1/2 Cups milk
1 1/2 Cups mashed potatoes

Directions
In a saucepan, melt butter and add in milk, water and mashed potatoes. Blend together.

In a mixer, add together sugar, salt, yeast and four Cups flour. Add warm mashed potatoes mixture, just make sure it isn't too hot just warm.

Blend in mashed potatoes in mixer. Add in 2 eggs. Mix in three cups flour one cup at a time mixing together well.

Knead and place dough in a greased bowl. Cover with a towel or plastic wrap and let rise about 1 hour. Punch dough down and knead gently. Let rise again about 20 minutes. Form dough into rolls and place on a greased cookie sheet. Bake in a preheated oven at 400 degrees for 35-40 minutes until golden brown.

How to Shape Rolls

Any basic white, wheat or herb bread recipe can be used to make breads or breadsticks. After your dough rise the first time, shape your bread dough in whatever fashion you'd like. Then let rise about 20-30 minutes and bake.

Cloverleaf rolls-Place three small balls of dough together in a muffin tin.

Fan tans- Roll dough out in the shape of a rectangle. Then cut strips about 1inch wide. Stack strips and place in a muffin tin with the cut ends up.

Snail roll- Roll a piece of bread dough into a long rope. Coil dough rope into a spiral.

Bow ties- - Roll a piece of bread dough into a long rope. Tie rope into a knot and pull the ends through.

Soft Pretzels-- Roll a piece of bread dough into a long rope. With the ends of the rope make an X at the top. Bring ends down in the shape of a pretzel.

To **make butter horns,** roll dough into large circles. Brush dough with melted butter. Cut dough into large wedges with a pizza cutter or knife. Roll each wedge towards the pointed end. (like croissants)

Homemade Bagels

Ingredients
1 2/3 Cups warm water
1/4 Cup white sugar
2 tsp salt
5 Cups white flour
1 T. yeast

Directions
In a mixing bowl, dissolve yeast in warm water and sprinkle with sugar. Add in salt and flour and blend until a smooth ball of dough. Place in a greased bowl and let rise one hour. Split dough into four equal balls. With each ball split into three balls of bough. Press a hole in the center of each ball of dough and shape into a bagel shape.

In a large pot, boil water to fill 3/4 full and add 2 Tablespoons sugar. Drop bagels into boiling water and let boil 3-5 minutes. Take out of water and place on a greased cookie sheet. Continue with all of dough and bake in a preheated oven for 20-25 minutes until golden brown.

Orange Rolls

Bread dough enough to make about 16 balls of dough

Ingredients

1/3 Cup butter, melted
1/2 Cup white sugar
1 tsp. cinnamon
2-3 T. orange peel, grated

Directions

In a small bowl, mix sugar and orange peel together. Roll bread dough in about 16 balls. Dip each piece of dough into melted butter and then in sugar mixture. Place balls of dough into greased Bundt pan. Bake in a preheated oven at 350 degrees for 30-35 minutes.

Optional Glaze

1 1/2 T. orange juice mix until smooth with 1/2 Cup powdered sugar. Pour over warm rolls.

Monkey Bread

Bread dough enough to make about 16-20 balls of dough

Ingredients
1/2 Cup butter
1 Cup brown sugar
1 T. cinnamon
3 T. milk

Directions

Grease a Bundt pan. Roll bread dough into balls. Place in layers in the pan. In microwave safe dish, add butter, sugar, cinnamon and milk. Cook one minute or until butter is melted.

Pour mixture over bread dough. Bake in a preheated oven at 375 degrees for about 30 minutes or until golden brown.

Pull Apart Bacon Bread

Ingredients

12 bacon strips, diced
1 loaf (1 pound) frozen bread dough, thawed
2 T. vegetable oil
1 Cup mozzarella cheese, shredded
1 envelope ranch salad dressing mix

Directions

Fry bacon until crispy and drain. Allow to cool and chop. Roll bread dough into small balls about the size of a quarter. In a large bowl, stir together chopped bacon, cheese, dressing mix and oil. Roll each ball in mixture and layer in a greased Bundt pan. Drizzle any leftover oil mixture over the top of dough.

Cover and let rise half hour. Bake in a preheated oven at 350 degrees for 20 minutes or until golden brown.

Herb Bread Sticks

Ingredients
1 pkg. yeast
1/4 Cup warm water
1 Tbsp. sugar
1/2 tsp. salt
2-3 Cups flour
2/3 Cup milk; warmed

Directions
In mixing bowl, dissolve yeast in warm water. Sprinkle sugar over the top and let sit several minutes. Add in milk, salt and 2 Cups flour. Blend together. If mixture is too sticky add more flour until forms a nice bowl and dough pulls away from sides of mixing bowl. Knead dough several minutes and place in a greased bowl. Cover with a towel and let sit until doubles in size.

Roll small pieces of dough into breadsticks and place on a greased cookie sheet.

Mix together:
1/3 Cup olive oil
2 cloves garlic, minced
1/4 Cup Parmesan cheese
2 T. Italian seasoning or mixed herbs

Brush mixture on to each breadstick. Let rise again about 20 minutes. Bake in a preheated oven at 375 degrees for 15-20 minutes until breadsticks are golden brown.

Breadsticks with Parmesan Butter
Ingredients
2 Pkgs. Yeast or 2 T. yeast
1/2 Cup white sugar
2 Cups warm water
3 T. vegetable oil
1 egg
1 tsp. salt
4 1/2- 5 Cups flour

Directions
In mixer bowl, dissolve yeast and 1 T. sugar in1 Cup warm water. Let sit several minutes; then add in oil, egg, salt, 2 Cups flour, and remaining sugar and water. Mix until well blended. Add more flour if needed to make a smooth ball of dough. Knead on floured surface. Place dough in greased bowl until doubles in size.
Roll pieces of dough into breadsticks and lay on greased cookie sheet. Cover and let rise 20 minutes. Bake in a preheated oven at 400 degrees for 10-12 minutes. or until golden brown.

Parmesan Butter for Dipping
1/2 Cup butter, softened
2 T. parmesan cheese
1 garlic clove, minced
Directions
Cream butter, parmesan cheese and garlic together and serve with warm breadsticks.

What to Do with Bread Dough

Besides have a fresh loaf of homemade bread, there are many things you can do with the bread dough instead of making loaves of bread. Breadsticks, dinner rolls or crescent rolls can accompany your meals.

Once you learn how to make bread dough, you can use the dough to create other fun creations like homemade bagels, English muffins, bread bowls for soup or center dinner around bread like Stromboli or stuffed chicken rolls.

Pizza Stromboli

Using bread dough, roll into a rectangle. Top with pizza toppings of your choice.

Roll up dough, jelly roll style. In a small bowl, beat one egg with 1 tsp. Italian seasoning and 1/2 tsp garlic salt. Blend together. Brush Stromboli with egg mixture. Bake in a preheated oven at 425 degrees F for 15-20 minutes or until golden brown.

Chicken Roll Ups

Ingredients
bread dough
2 Cups rotisserie chicken, shredded
8 oz. cream cheese
pinch of salt and pepper
1/4 Cup shredded cheese

Directions
In a bowl, mix together cream cheese, shredded cheese and cooked chicken. Season with salt and pepper.

Roll bread dough into a large circle. Cut with a pizza cutter into triangles. Add a spoonful of chicken mixture on each end of a triangle. Roll up starting from the long end. Place on greased cookie sheet. Preheat oven at 350 degrees F. Bake rolls for 10-15 minutes until golden brown.

In a bowl, blend together cooked chicken, cream cheese and cheese. Sprinkle with salt and pepper. Roll crescent dough out into a circle and cut into triangles or unroll dough if using store bought. Place chicken mixture on the end of each triangle.

Chicken Braid
Ingredients
Rotisserie chicken, shredded or chopped cooked chicken breasts
broccoli, chopped and cooked
1/2 Cup cheddar or Colby cheese, shredded
1/4-1/2 Cup mayonnaise
pinch of salt and pepper
bread dough

Directions
Roll bread dough out into a rectangle. In a large bowl, mix together chicken, broccoli, cheese, mayonnaise and salt and pepper. Adjust ingredients to taste. Lay chicken mixture in the middle of your rectangle.

Slit edges on both sides, making a fringe on both sides. Tie two opposite side fringes in a twist. Press ends together to seal. Bake at 400 degrees for 15-20 minutes until dough is golden brown.

Hamburger Rolls

Ingredients
Bread dough or frozen bread rolls
1 lb. beef, ground
salt and pepper
1 onion, chopped
shredded cabbage or coleslaw bag mix
egg white, for brushing tops

Directions
Brown beef in a skillet with chopped onion. Season with salt and pepper. Drain and put back into skillet. Stir in chopped cabbage. Cook several minutes until cabbage starts to wilt.

Press ball of dough into a flat circle. Add a spoonful of beef to roll and gather ends and press together. Place on a greased cookie sheet. Brush the top of each roll with beaten egg white.

Bake in a preheated oven at 350 degrees for 10-15 minutes until golden brown.

~If using a homemade bread dough recipe like the ones in this book, you may have some dough leftover after using all the beef mixture.

Meatball Rolls

This recipe is like the one previously but is a faster version.

Using cooked meatballs, wrap a meatball within a piece of bread dough and wrap ends together. Seal tightly and place on a greased cookie sheet. Brush tops with egg white and sprinkle with garlic salt or salt if desired. Bake in a preheated oven at 350 degrees for 10-15 minutes until golden brown.

Philly Steak Calzones

Try making these into individual or family size sandwiches.

Ingredients
bread dough
1 1/2 pounds steak strips or roast beef
1 can French onion soup
1/2 cup diced bell peppers (red, green, & yellow), finely diced
1/4 cup shredded cheese, your choice
pinch of salt and pepper

Directions
Preheat oven to 350 degrees. Cook meat in skillet and add can of soup. Season with salt and pepper and add in bell peppers. Cook until the liquid has been soaked up.

Roll dough into a large circle, if making individual sizes make small circles.

Add meat to middle of dough. Fold over as you would a calzone or fold like a taco. Seal edges by pressing together with a fork.

Place on greased cookie sheet and bake for 40-50 minutes until golden brown.

~Add shredded cheese to the mixture if desired.

Indian Fry Bread Tacos

Ingredients
homemade bread dough
refried beans
1 lb. Ground Beef, cooked
1 Cup or more cheddar cheese, shredded
Taco fixings of choice

Directions
Take small balls of dough and flat into round patties. Add small amount of oil in frying pan and heat. Fry bread dough on both sides until golden brown. Drain on a paper towel.

To serve, top your fry bread with taco fixings. We like to add chili or beans, beef, cheese, lettuce, tomatoes and sour cream.

Cinnamon Knots

Ingredients
2 Cups milk warmed
2 Tbsp yeast or one pkg
1/2 Cup warm water
1/2 Cup butter, melted
1/4 Cup white sugar
2 eggs, well beaten
5-6 Cups all-purpose flour
1 1/2 Cups sugar
3 T. cinnamon
1 Cup butter, melted

Directions
Warm milk in a microwave safe dish until it is just warm but not too hot. In a small bowl, dissolve yeast in warm water and sprinkle a pinch of sugar over the top. Let sit several minutes.

In a mixer, add eggs, butter, sugar and salt. Blend together until creamy. Add in warm milk. Make sure the mixture is not too hot to kill the yeast, if too hot let cool. Add in yeast and 2 Cups flour. Blend together. Continue to add in remaining flour until dough forms a ball and pulls away from sides of mixing bowl.

Knead about 5 minutes and place in a greased bowl. Let rise one hour.

Mix together 1 1/2 Cups sugar and 3 T. cinnamon. Set aside. Roll dough into a rectangle and cut into long strips. Dip each strip in one cup melted butter and then dip in cinnamon and sugar mixture.

Tie each strip in a loose knot and place on a greased cookie sheet. Bake in a preheated oven at 350 degrees for 15-20 minutes until golden brown.

Cinnamon Rolls

Ingredients

2 Tablespoons yeast
1 /4 cup warm water (105 to 115 degrees F)
1 1/2 cups warm milk
1/2 cup granulated sugar
1 teaspoon salt
2 eggs
1/3 cup shortening
5 cups all-purpose flour, divided
1/4-1/2 Cup melted butter
brown sugar
cinnamon
vanilla or cream cheese frosting, prepared or store bought

Directions

In a glass measuring cup, add yeast and warm water. Sprinkle top with a pinch of sugar. This helps "feed" the yeast. Set aside. In mixing bowl, add warm milk, sugar, salt, eggs and shortening. Blend together. Add in 2 cups flour and continue to blend. Pour in yeast mixture and add remaining flour. Mix together until dough forms into a ball. Knead several minutes on a floured counter. Let rest 30 minutes.

Roll dough into a large rectangle. Spread with 1/4 Cup melted butter. Sprinkle entire surface of dough with sugar and cinnamon. Massage sugar into butter. Roll up jelly roll style. Cut in 1-inch slices and place on a greased baking sheet. Bake at 350 degrees for 15-20 minutes until lightly golden brown. Spread prepared frosting over top of warm rolls.

Bread Bowls

Bread bowls are fun to serve soups or dips in

1. To make bowls, lightly crush sheets of foil into 3½-inch balls. Set the balls onto cookie sheets. Press or roll a ball of dough to a 5-inch circle. Place each bread dough circle over a foil ball, shaping gently to fit around the foil and form a bowl shape, making sure dough doesn't touch the cookie sheet.

2. Using homemade bread dough, divide into balls of dough to make large rolls.   Let rise until double in size. Bake rolls in a preheated oven at 350 degrees for 20-25 minutes or until golden brown. Allow to cool. Slice off the top of each roll and scoop out bread filling. Save the bread for bread crumbs or croutons for another meal.